Note Speller

by EDWARD JANOWSKY

A SYSTEMATIZED SET OF WORK SHEETS
FOR SUPPLEMENTING ANY ELEMENTARY CLASS OR PRIVATE METHOD.

DESIGNED TO HELP THE STUDENT GAIN A BETTER UNDERSTANDING OF THE PROBLEMS
OF FINGERING AND READING MUSIC AND AT THE SAME TIME SAVE VALUABLE LESSON TIME.

Published for:
Flute and Piccolo (EL00462)
Clarinet (EL00448)
Oboe (EL00463)
Bassoon (EL00464)
Saxophone (EL00451)

Trumpet (Baritone T.C.) (EL00449)
French Horn (EL00465)
Trombone (EL00450)
Baritone B.C. (EL00467)
Tuba (EL00468)
Drum Rhythm Speller (EL01063)

Foreword

The writing lessons in this book are designed to develop the viola student's knowledge of the letter names and fingerings of all natural notes which can be played in the first position.

With the aid of proven "write to remember" technics the student will be able to master these fundamentals with a minimum amount of assistance. This will enable the instructor to concentrate more fully on other aspects of viola playing.

The objectives of this book do not include the teaching of note values, time signatures, measures or bar lines. However, all of these symbols have been presented in the lessons as they are used in a normal playing situation. As the student learns to play, there will be no conflict between the music he has encountered in his writing exercises and that which he actually performs.

This book should be of special value to those advanced violin students who wish to acquire a working knowledge of viola notes and fingerings.

Contents

EL 440

THE VIOLA

Memorize the names of these important parts of the viola . They are referred to later in the book.

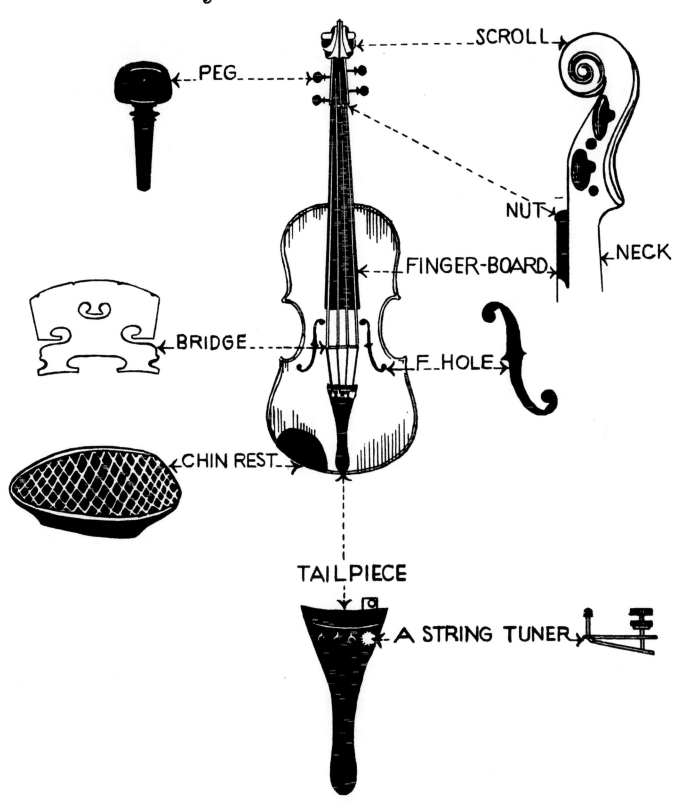

SCROLL

PEG

NUT

NECK

FINGER-BOARD

BRIDGE

F. HOLE

CHIN REST

TAILPIECE

A STRING TUNER

THE STAFF
5 LINES AND 4 SPACES

Notes and rests are placed on the FIVE LINES or in the FOUR SPACES of the STAFF.

1 Write the NUMBER of the LINE or SPACE on which each of the following notes is placed.

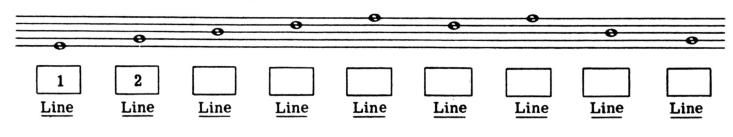

1	2							
Line	Line	Line	Line	Line	Line	Line	Line	Line

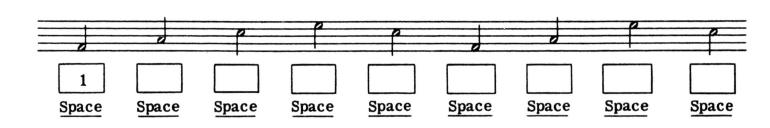

1								
Space	Space	Space	Space	Space	Space	Space	Space	Space

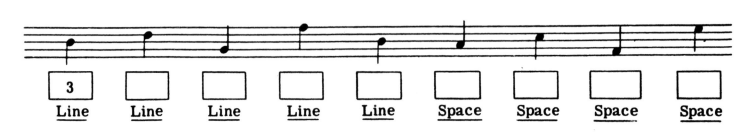

3								
Line	Line	Line	Line	Line	Space	Space	Space	Space

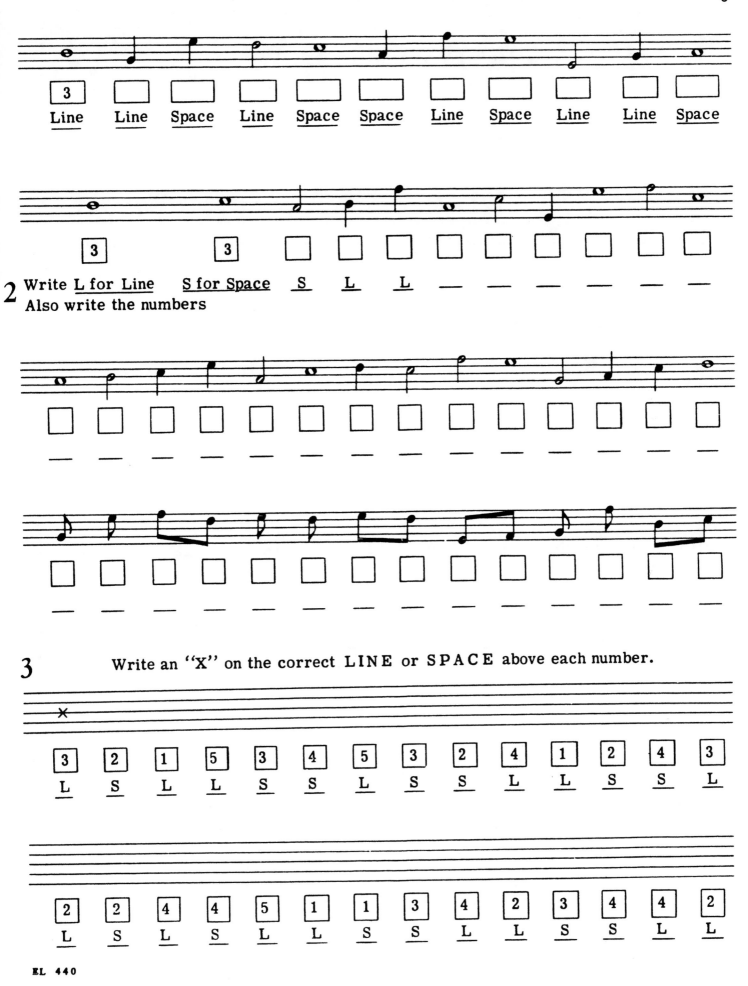

3   Write an "X" on the correct LINE or SPACE above each number.

LINES AND SPACES ABOVE THE STAFF

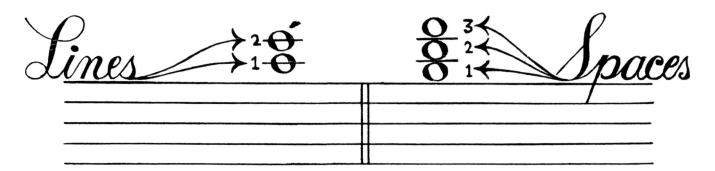

The lines above and below the staff are known as LEGER LINES. Music written for the viola may use as many as FOUR LEGER LINES ABOVE the STAFF.

1   Write in the NUMBER of the LEGER LINE or SPACE on which each of the following notes is placed. "ABOVE" is used for "above the staff."

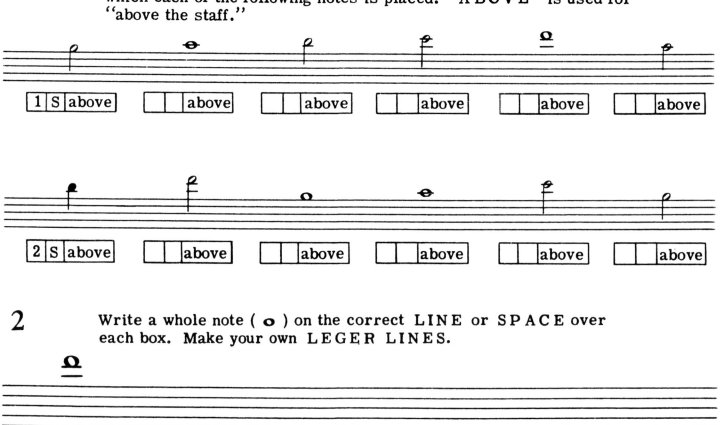

2   Write a whole note (o) on the correct LINE or SPACE over each box. Make your own LEGER LINES.

LINES AND SPACES BELOW THE STAFF

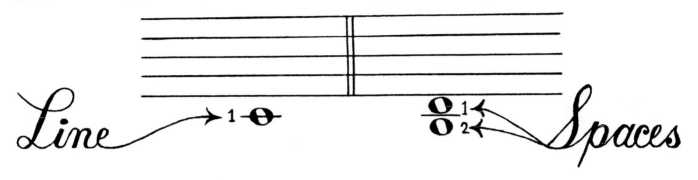

1 Write in the N U M B E R of the L I N E or S P A C E on which each of the following notes is placed. The word "below" is used for "below the staff."

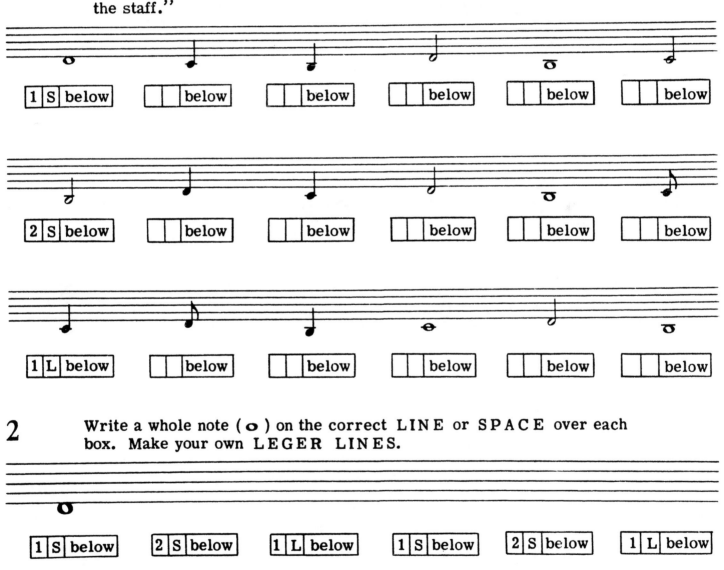

2 Write a whole note (o) on the correct L I N E or S P A C E over each box. Make your own L E G E R L I N E S.

Note: Viola music written in the alto clef makes use of only one leger line below the staff.

ALTO CLEF
ON THE STAFF

The ALTO CLEF sign is usually found at the beginning of each staff of viola music.

As you learn more about the viola, you will become acquainted with the TREBLE CLEF which is sometimes used for viola music.

When drawing our own clefs, we use a simplified version.

1   Draw over the dotted lines shown below.

Step One   *Step Two*

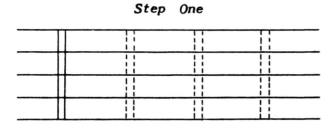   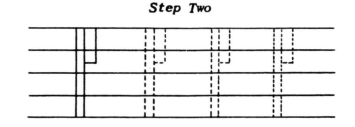

Step Three

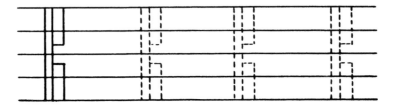

2 Complete each **A L T O   C L E F.**

3 Draw a complete **A L T O   C L E F** on each staff.

4 Draw **A L T O   C L E F S** on each staff and write in a whole note on the correct **L I N E** or **S P A C E** over each box. Make your own leger lines.

2 S   3 L   2 S above

2 S below   5 L   1 L below

1 L above   4 S   2 S

1 L above   2 S   3 S   2 L

OPEN STRINGS AND THEIR LETTER NAMES

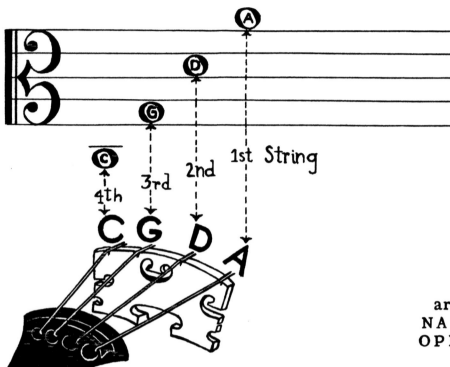

C, G, D, and A
are the LETTER
NAMES of the four
OPEN STRINGS.

Occasionally the OPEN STRINGS are given NUMBER NAMES from the highest to the lowest (1st, 2nd, 3rd, and 4th strings) as shown in the illustrations.

1 Draw a line from each OPEN STRING note to its LETTER NAME or STRING NUMBER NAME on the bridge.

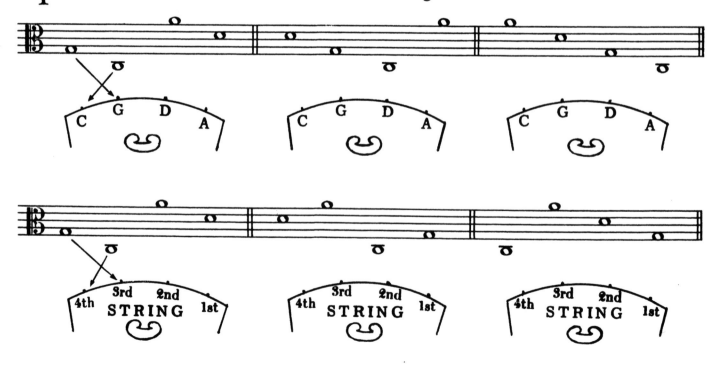

2 Write in the LETTER NAMES of the following OPEN STRING NOTES.

3 Circle the OPEN STRING NOTES on the following staves and write in their LETTER NAMES on the dotted lines. "Staves" is the plural of staff.

TUNING THE VIOLA

D is the first white key to the left of the piano **KEY HOLE**. The other open strings are found by counting up five white keys or down five white keys. Always count the note you start from as "number one".

If you play piano you may find your notes from "MIDDLE C."

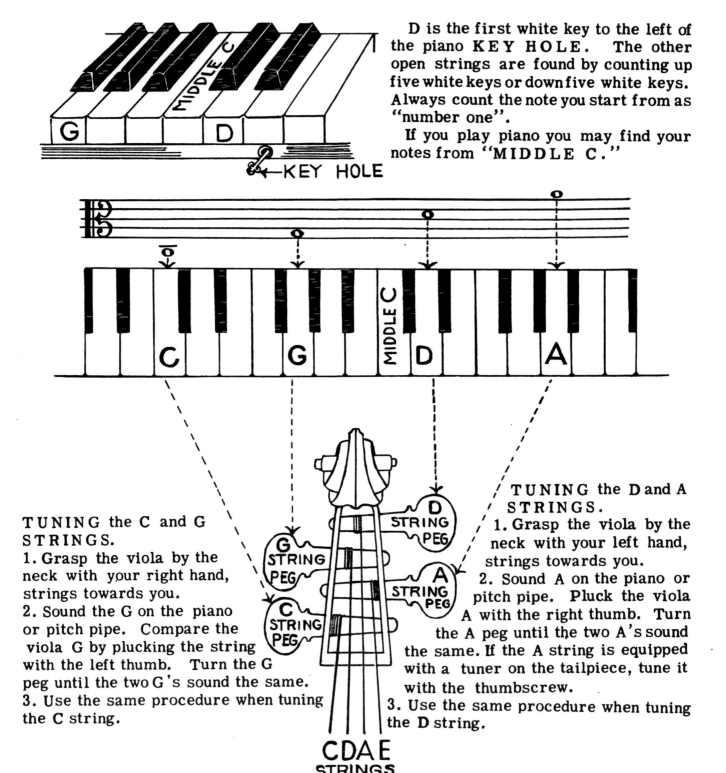

TUNING the C and G STRINGS.

1. Grasp the viola by the neck with your right hand, strings towards you.
2. Sound the G on the piano or pitch pipe. Compare the viola G by plucking the string with the left thumb. Turn the G peg until the two G's sound the same.
3. Use the same procedure when tuning the C string.

TUNING the D and A STRINGS.

1. Grasp the viola by the neck with your left hand, strings towards you.
2. Sound A on the piano or pitch pipe. Pluck the viola A with the right thumb. Turn the A peg until the two A's sound the same. If the A string is equipped with a tuner on the tailpiece, tune it with the thumbscrew.
3. Use the same procedure when tuning the D string.

4. Turn the pegs away from you to raise the pitch.
5. When turning pegs push them into the scroll.
6. The A string is usually tuned first. D, G and C may be tuned in the same manner.

1 Fill in the name of each unmarked TUNING PEG on its dotted line.

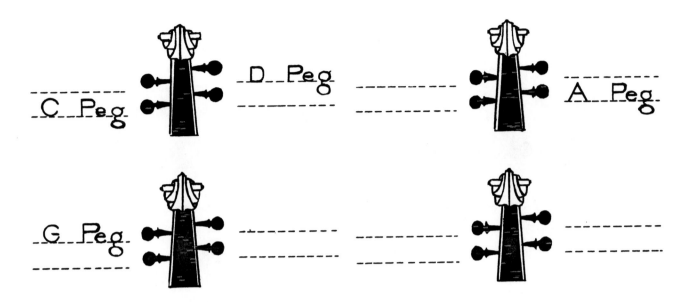

2 Draw a line from each OPEN STRING NOTE to its TUNING PEG.

3 Locate the four OPEN STRING NOTES on the PIANO KEYBOARD and mark each one with its LETTER NAME.

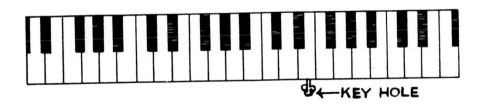

KEY HOLE

EL 440

NOTES AND 1st 2nd 3rd 4th FINGERS ON THE A STRING
(First String)

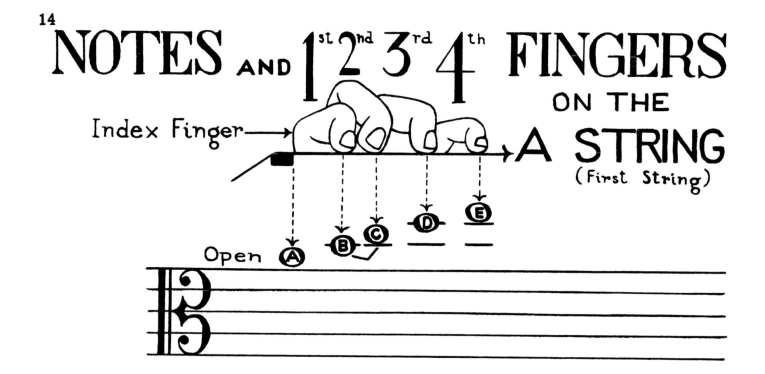

Index Finger →

The notes B and C are close together or a HALF-STEP apart. The bracket (⌃) as shown in the illustration is used to mark the HALF-STEP. The OPEN STRING is indicated by an "O".

1 Write in the LETTER NAMES of the following A STRING NOTES and mark each HALF-STEP with a bracket (⌃).

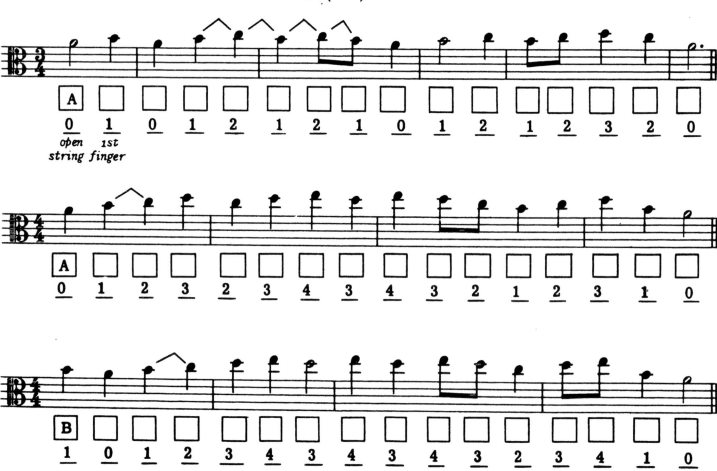

A															
0	1	0	1	2	1	2	1	0	1	2	1	2	3	2	0

open — 1st
string finger

A															
0	1	2	3	2	3	4	3	4	3	2	1	2	3	1	0

B															
1	0	1	2	3	4	3	4	3	4	3	2	3	4	1	0

EL 440

2 Write in the FINGERINGS of the following A STRING NOTES and mark each HALF-STEP with a bracket (⌒).

3 Write in the LETTER NAMES and FINGERINGS of the following A STRING NOTES. Mark the HALF-STEPS.

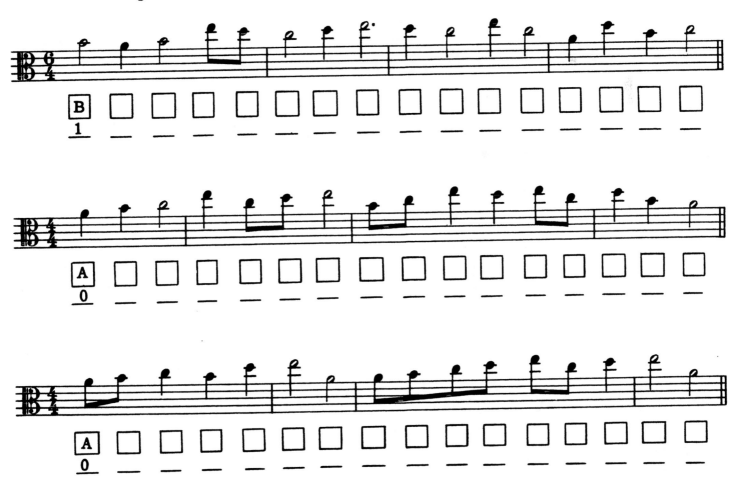

EL 440

4 Circle the **A STRING NOTES** on the following staves and write in their **LETTER NAMES** and **FINGERINGS** on the dotted lines. The plural of "staff" is staves.

5 Write in the correct **LETTER NAMES** and **FINGERINGS** of the following **A STRING NOTES**, and musical words will appear.

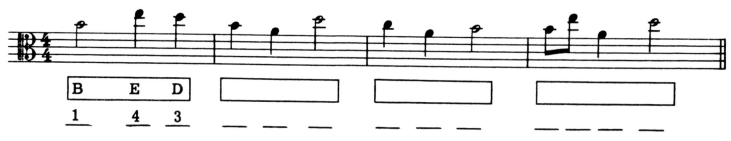

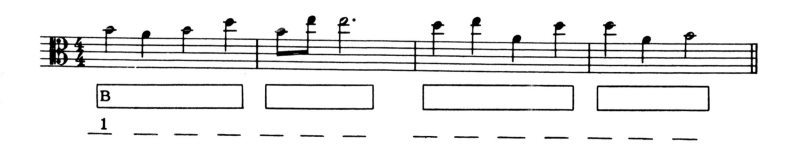

6   Write in the **A STRING NOTES** and their **LETTER NAMES** as indicated by the given fingerings. Use whole notes.

A										
0	1	2	3	4	3	1	2	0	3	1

B										
1	3	2	4	1	0	2	4	1	0	3

7   Write in the **A STRING NOTES** and their **FINGERINGS** as indicated by the given letter names. Use whole notes.

A	B	D	C	E	B	A	D	B	C	A
0	—	—	—	—	—	—	—	—	—	—

C	A	E	B	A	B	E	A	D	B	E
2	—	—	—	—	—	—	—	—	—	—

EL 440

NOTES AND 1ˢᵗ 2ⁿᵈ 3ʳᵈ 4ᵗʰ FINGERS ON THE D STRING
(second String)

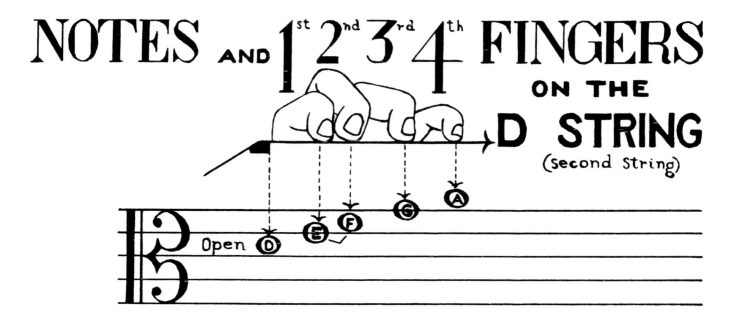

The fingers used to play the notes E and F are always placed close together or a HALF-STEP apart. The bracket (⌒ or ⌄) marks this HALF-STEP.

After the notes and fingers on the D string have been learned, the explanation on page 21 will show you when to use the 4th finger A or the open A.

1   Write in the LETTER NAMES of the following D STRING NOTES and mark the HALF-STEPS.

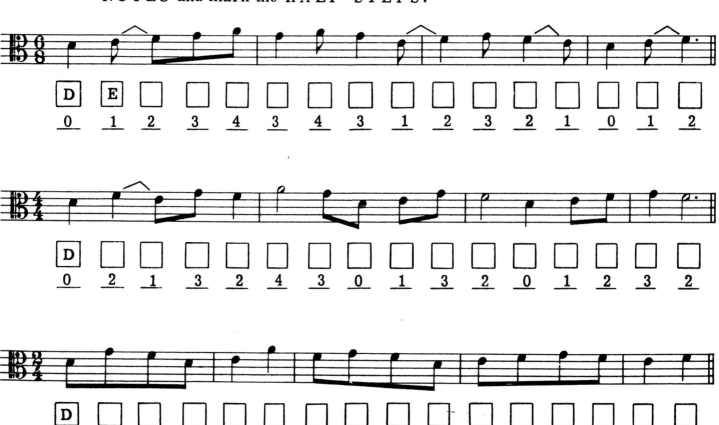

2 Write in the FINGERINGS of the following D STRING NOTES and mark each HALF-STEP.

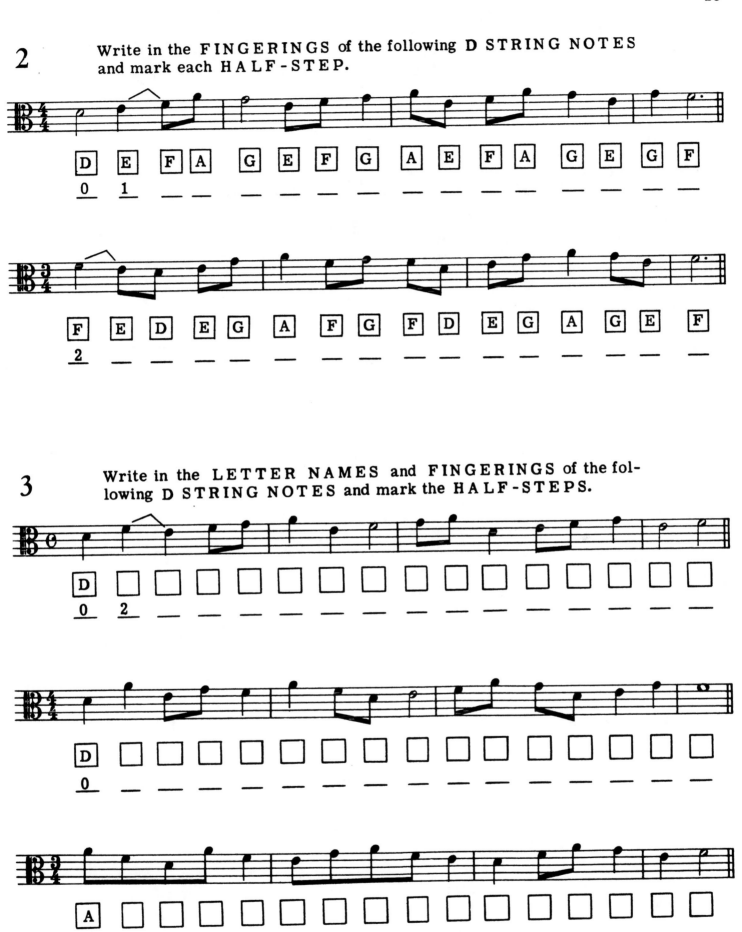

3 Write in the LETTER NAMES and FINGERINGS of the following D STRING NOTES and mark the HALF-STEPS.

4 Circle the **D STRING NOTES** on the following staves. Write in their **LETTER NAMES** and **FINGERINGS** on the dotted lines.

D E
0 1

D
0

5 Write in the **D STRING NOTES** and their **FINGERINGS** as indicated by the given letter names. Use whole notes.

D E F G A E G A D F G
0 — — — — — — — — — —

F D G E A D F G E A E
2 — — — — — — — — — —

G A E D F A F A D E A
3 — — — — — — — — — —

OPEN A AND 4th FINGER A

When the A on the 1st space above the staff is preceded and followed by D STRING notes (D, E, F, or G), use the 4th FINGER A.

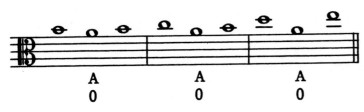

When the A on the 1st space above the staff is preceded and followed by A STRING notes (B, C, D, or E), use the OPEN A.

When going UP from the D string to the A string in a scale passage, use the OPEN A. When going down, use the 4th FINGER A.

1 Write in the LETTER NAMES and FINGERINGS of the following D and A STRING NOTES.

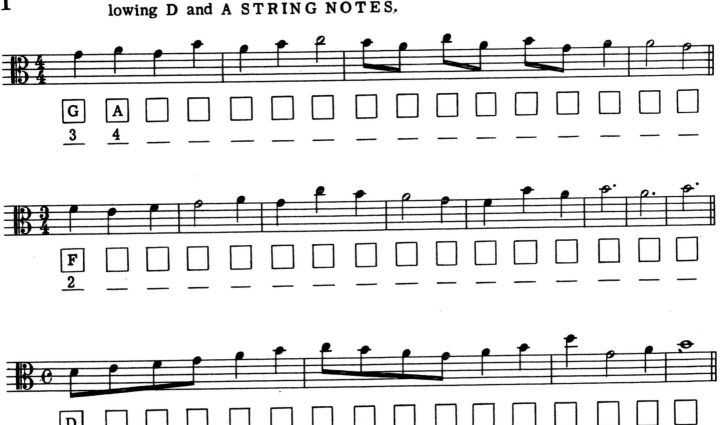

NOTES AND 1st 2nd 3rd 4th FINGERS ON THE G STRING
(Third String)

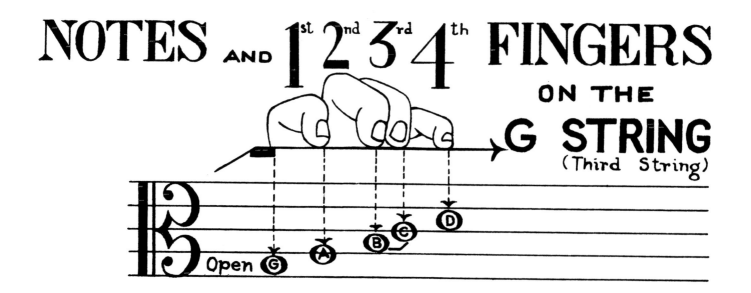

The fingers used to play the notes **B** and **C** are always placed close together or a H A L F - S T E P apart. This bracket(⌢) marks each H A L F - S T E P. All **D**'s for the next three pages are "4th FIN-GER **D**'s."

1   Write in the LETTER NAMES of the following G STRING NOTES and mark the HALF-STEPS.

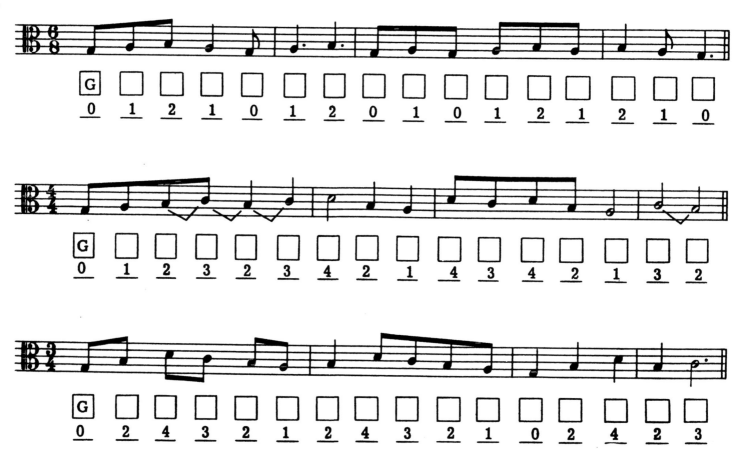

2 Write in the FINGERINGS of the following G STRING NOTES and mark each HALF-STEP.

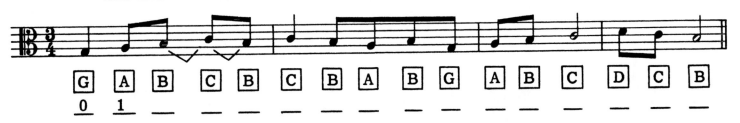

G A B C B C B A B G A B C D C B
0 1 _ _ _ _ _ _ _ _ _ _ _ _ _ _

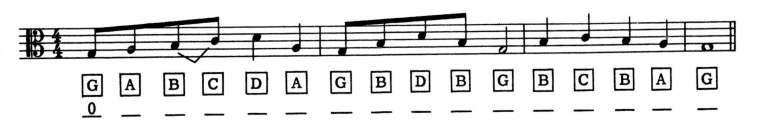

G A B C D A G B D B G B C B A G
0 _ _ _ _ _ _ _ _ _ _ _ _ _ _ _

3 Write in the LETTER NAMES and FINGERINGS of the following G STRING NOTES. Mark the HALF-STEPS.

B
2 _ _ _ _ _ _ _ _ _ _ _ _ _ _

B
2 _ _ _ _ _ _ _ _ _ _ _ _ _ _

D
4 _ _ _ _ _ _ _ _ _ _ _ _ _ _

EL 440

24

4   Circle the G STRING NOTES on the following staves. Write in their LETTER NAMES and FINGERINGS on the dotted lines.

G   B
- -
0   2
- -

G
- -
0
- -

5   Write in the G STRING NOTES and their FINGERINGS as indicated by the given letter names. Use whole notes.

G	B	C	A	D	C	A	G	D	B	G
0	—	—	—	—	—	—	—	—	—	—

G	D	A	C	G	B	D	C	A	D	G
0	—	—	—	—	—	—	—	—	—	—

B	D	C	A	G	C	D	B	G	A	C
2	—	—	—	—	—	—	—	—	—	—

EL 440

OPEN D AND 4th FINGER D

When the 3rd space D is preceded and followed by G STRING notes (G, A, B, or C), use the 4th FINGER D.

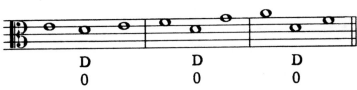

When the 3rd space D is preceded and followed by D STRING notes (E, F, G, or A), use the OPEN D.

When going UP from the G string to the D string in a scale passage, use the OPEN D. When going down, use the 4th FINGER D.

1 Write in the LETTER NAMES and FINGERINGS of the following G and D STRING NOTES.

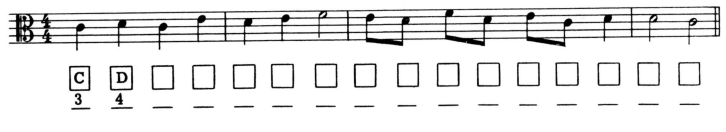

NOTES AND 1ˢᵗ 2ⁿᵈ 3ʳᵈ 4ᵗʰ FINGERS
ON THE
C STRING
(Fourth String)

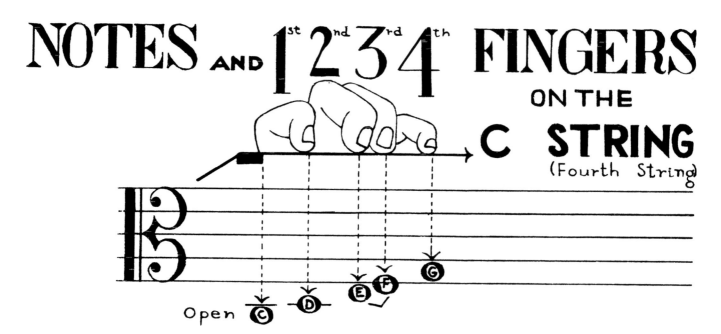

The fingers used to play the notes E and F are always placed close together or a HALF-STEP apart. The bracket (⌒) marks the HALF-STEP. All G's for the next three pages are "4th FINGER G's".

1 Write in the LETTER NAMES of the following C STRING NOTES and mark the HALF-STEPS.

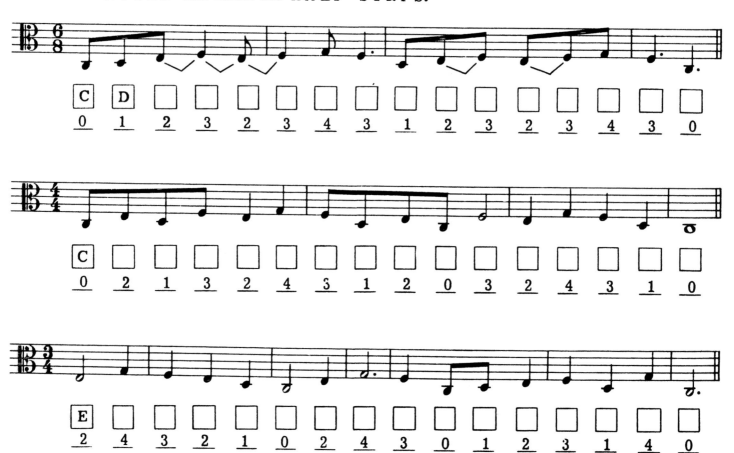

2 Write in the FINGERINGS of the following C STRING NOTES and mark each HALF-STEP with a bracket (⌒).

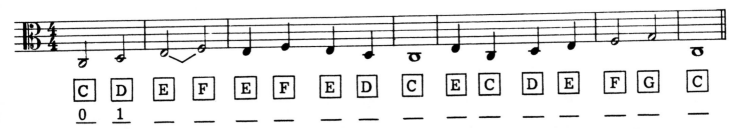

3 Write in the LETTER NAMES and FINGERINGS of the following C STRING NOTES. Mark the HALF-STEPS.

4 Circle the C STRING NOTES on the following staves. Write in the LETTER NAMES and FINGERINGS on the dotted lines.

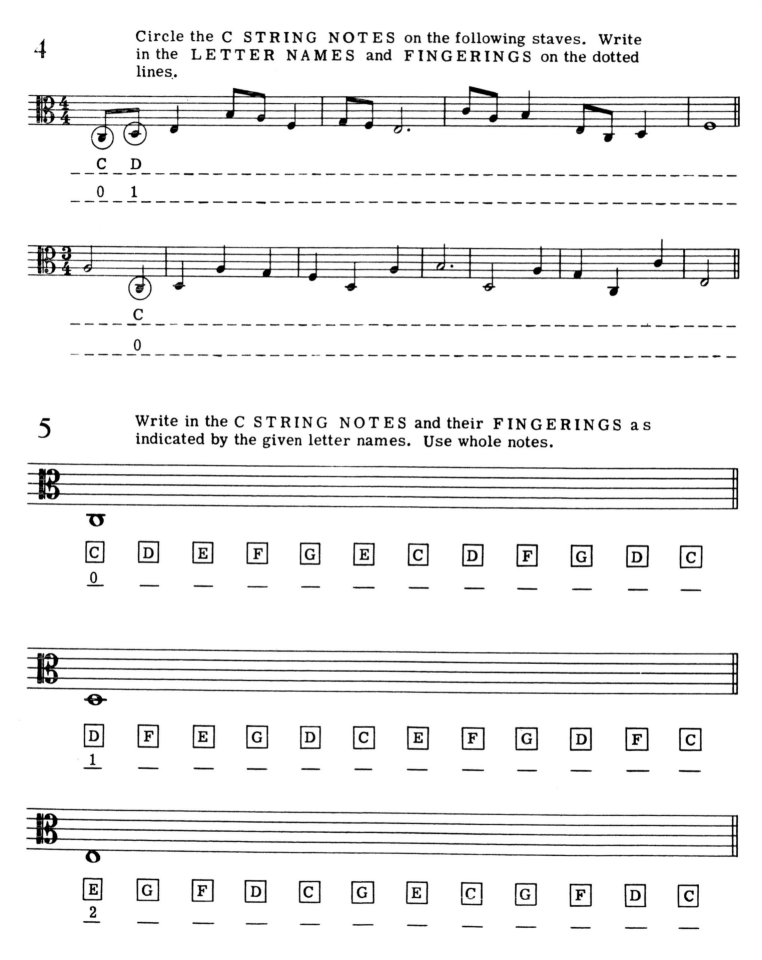

5 Write in the C STRING NOTES and their FINGERINGS as indicated by the given letter names. Use whole notes.

OPEN G AND 4th FINGER G

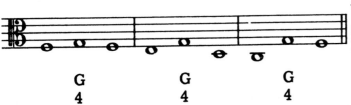

When the G (1st space on the staff) is preceded and followed by C STRING notes (C, D, E, or F), use the 4th FINGER G.

When the G (1st space on the staff) is preceded and followed by G STRING notes (A, B, C, or D), use the OPEN G.

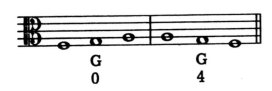

When going UP from the C string to the G string in a scale passage, use the OPEN G. When going down, use the 4th FINGER G.

1 Write in the LETTER NAMES and FINGERINGS of the following C and G STRING NOTES.

NOTES AND FINGERS ON FOUR STRINGS

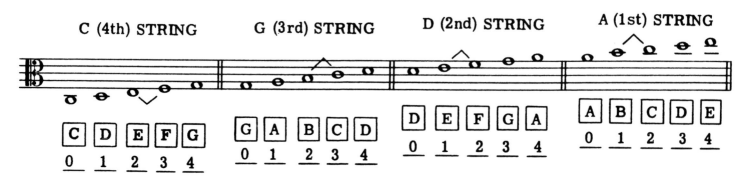

The above illustration shows all of the notes in the key of C which can be played in the first position.

1 Write in the LETTER NAMES and FINGERINGS of the following notes. Mark each HALF-STEP with a bracket.

2 Write in the LETTER NAMES and FINGERINGS of the following C, G, D, and A STRING notes. Mark the HALF-STEPS.

3 Write in the LETTER NAMES and FINGERINGS of the following notes and musical words will appear.

RELATED FINGER POSITIONS
ON THE FOUR STRINGS

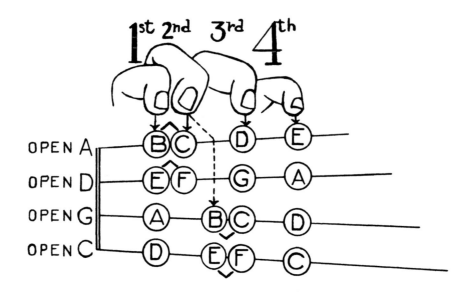

The above diagram shows the finger positions of all natural notes in the first position. It is easy to see from this diagram that the distance from any finger to any other finger (except when using the second finger B or second finger E) is the same on all four strings.

The notes and fingerings taught in this book are not the only ones you will use. As your knowledge of the viola increases, your instructor will introduce you to sharps (♯) and flats (♭). You will also learn about additional leger lines above the staff and how to move your left hand into "the higher positions." This will enable you to play many new notes such as the following:

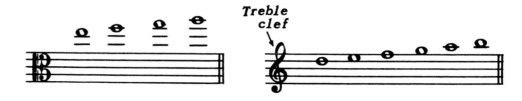